THE BARRON HOUSE SOUPS

HEART-FRIENDLY SOUPS FOR GREAT FIRST IMPRESSIONS

RECIPES FOR SOUPS SERVED IN THIS HISTORIC COUNTRY HOTEL WITH INGREDIENTS ADJUSTED TO KEEP CHOLESTEROL AND FAT AT A MINIMUM, BUT THE TASTE LIKE THE ORIGINAL

BY

JOHN BOHUMIL

authorHOUSE

1663 LIBERTY DRIVE, SUITE 200
BLOOMINGTON, INDIANA 47403
(800) 839-8640
WWW.AUTHORHOUSE.COM

© 2004 John Bohumil.
All Rights Reserved.

No part of this book may be reproduced, stored in a retrieval system, or transmitted by any means without the written permission of the author.

First published by AuthorHouse 09/20/04

ISBN: 1-4184-9678-2 (e)
ISBN: 1-4184-9677-4 (sc)

Printed in the United States of America
Bloomington, Indiana

This book is printed on acid-free paper.

TABLE OF CONTENTS

ABOUT THE BARRON HOUSE AND ITS FOODS 1
    SO WHY IS THIS COLLECTION OF RECIPES FOCUSED ON SOUPS? 3

ABOUT INGREDIENTS AND MEASUREMENTS 5

A FEW ABBREVIATIONS I WILL USE 7

ABOUT ASPARAGUS 9
    INSPIRING ASPARAGUS SOUP 11
    BACON AND EGG DROP SOUP 13
    "BEAN AND OTHER" SOUP 14
    BODACIOUS BROCCOLI SOUP 15
    BROWN SOUP 16
    BEEF BROTH SOUPS 17
        BEEF WITH RICE AND POTATOES SOUP 17
        BEEF WITH BARLEY SOUP 17
        BEEF WITH CREAM OF WHEAT SOUP 18
        BEEF WITH EGG DROP SOUP 18
    STALE BREAD BEEF SOUP 19
    BOHEMIAN ALPHABET SOUP 20
    CREDIBLE CAULI-BROC SOUP 21
    CLASSY CABBAGE SOUP 22
    NON-FAT CHICKEN NOODLE SOUP 23
    CAPTIVATING CARROT SOUP 24
    CHARD AND CARROT SOUP 25
    CELERY-SPINACH CREAM SOUP 26
    CHEESE AND ONION SOUP 27
    COOL CUCUMBER SOUP 28
    CUCUMBER CREAM SOUP 30
    CURRY WATER SOUP 31
    GRACIOUS GREEN HAM SOUP 32
    GLORIOUS GREEN PEA SOUP 33

GYPSY SOUP	34
LUMINOUS LETTUCE SOUP	36
LUSTROUS LEEK SOUP	37
MARBLE SOUP	38
MANIFOLD MATZO SOUP	39
MEAGER MEAT SOUP	41
MISTER T'S WHITE CRAB SOUP	43
MINI-MUSHROOM SOUP	45
NUSSBAUM'S GONE FISHING SOUP	46
BOHEMIAN POTATO SOUP	48
PRETENTIOUS PUMPKIN SOUP	50
RED CRAB SOUP	51
RED CHOWDER	52
SMOKY ONION SOUP	54
SPINACH ESCAROLE SOUP	56
SIMMERED SPLIT PEA SOUP	57
SQUISHY SQUASH SOUP	59
SWISS CHARD SOUP	60
SURPRISING SAUSAGE SOUP	61
ABOUT TOMATOES	63
THE TOMATO SOUP	64
FRESH TOMATO SOUP	65
SUPERB TOMATO SOUP	66
WINTER SQUASH SOUP	67
THE GREAT DEPRESSION	69
BARLEY SOUP	71
CHIPPED BEEF SOUP	72
PRETZEL SOUP	73
RIVEL SOUP	74
TOMATO MUSHROOM SOUP	75
'WHITHER THE BARRON HOUSE	76
THANKSGIVING CORN CHOWDER	77
A GENERAL NOSTALGIC POSTSCRIPT	79

ABOUT THE BARRON HOUSE AND ITS FOODS

Stagecoach lines were first established in the United States in the middle 1700's. The earliest routes connected Boston, New York City, and Philadelphia.

The Barron House was one of the stops on the stagecoach route north from Philadelphia. The horses were changed there before the climb over the Lehigh Mountains into Allentown and again on the return trip. Passengers would disembark to take care of personal needs and to eat in the Barron House dining room while the change was being made.

During the years before 1900 the Barron House cuisine was a combination of Pennsylvania Dutch and Amish. Beer, wine and whiskey helped to take the bumps out of the rutted roadway the stagecoaches navigated.

After the stagecoaches stopped running, the road on which the Barron House was located became a designated state route handling the early automobiles as well as horse drawn wagons. Eventually, an electric-powered trolley car was added on tracks laid in the center of the road and carried passengers between Philadelphia and Allentown.

The Barron House clientele also changed. Travelers still stopped for food and *now* for gasoline, and also water for their radiators or horses. However, a significant portion of the Barron House's customers were permanent or extended-stay residents in its hotel rooms who took all their meals in-house. Itinerant work crews stringing electric and telephone wires and building roads in the area, would also live and eat in the hotel. Other individuals working in the town and living in rented rooms also found the hotel's food attractive in both taste and cost, and patronized the Barron House.

And there were the banquets. Various organizations like the local bank used the hotel's large dining room for festive occasions. In those days of no air conditioning the large overhead fans and massive horse chestnut trees just outside made the room cool in summer and the central heating system made it cozy in winter.

Finally, in a day when most workers carried bag lunches, the hotel's boarding house style hot lunches attracted workers from the clothing factory just down the street and from other nearby employments, by the combination of quality and low price.

In the early 1900's a new owner and proprietor of the Barron House, originally from Bohemia, added Bohemian cuisine to the Dutch and Amish fare.

In Europe, Bohemia was a vigorous, long-established kingdom with a varietal and polished epicurean heritage. The Bohemian nobility was actually a prolific class and constituted a substantial segment of the Bohemian population. It sanctioned gentility and good living for itself *and* for the lower classes, providing education and skills enlargement for everyone.

When absorbed into the Austrian Empire, Bohemia kept its culture, its values, and its foods. The addition of Bohemian foods to the Barron House menu was very pleasing to the new Barron House clientele. After all, most of them ate every meal there and liked the variety.

SO WHY IS THIS COLLECTION OF RECIPES FOCUSED ON SOUPS?

Consider that most meals served after the stagecoach era at the Barron House were served to individuals who took all their 21 weekly meals there and to workers who ate all their week-day lunches there. These individuals were almost all men. Most of them did strenuous physical work for their living. For them every meal meant fueling up for the labors to come. They expected abundant bread, butter, and courses from soup to dessert, preferably pie.

The new proprietor was astute and a logical thinker. He made it a rule of the Barron House that the first course served, soup, include all the refills the patrons wanted. He reasoned that when you serve the same people 21 meals a week, it makes good sense to make the beginning of those meals a compelling experience.

If the soup was abundant and exceptionally tasty, he was convinced that the rest of the meal would be favorably colored by that initial impression. The soups *were* exceptional and their recipes should be available to posterity.

In putting together this collection of recipes I have endeavored to preserve their original taste, but with ingredients that will make the soups fully acceptable to those of us who must worry about keeping cholesterol low, HDL high, LDL low, and fat at a minimum.

The recipes meet that test. You will be serving Barron House soups very much as they tasted eighty to ninety years ago, but without cholesterol and fat.

ABOUT INGREDIENTS AND MEASUREMENTS

Soups are really works of art. If you've ever noticed that different batches of commercial V-8 juice vary in taste, you are privy to the fact that putting together the same ingredients may or may not get exactly the same taste you had before. So I offer you Rule 1.

1. *Always taste what you make and adjust ingredients and their amounts to get the taste that tastes good to you.*

The Barron House soups were dependent on seasonal ingredients. Vegetables grown in the Barron House's extensive garden varied in taste from one growing season to another. So, Rule 2.

2. *Follow the recipes but expect a little variance from time to time. And take heart from the fact that the differences are not caused by you but by nature.*

I had one major problem in up-dating the recipes for a health conscious age. The Barron House used traditional home-made beef and chicken broths. These are just too fatty for use now. I experimented with many substitutes. The very best I found are two powdery products called <u>G. Washington's Rich Brown Seasoning and Broth</u> and <u>G. Washington's Golden Seasoning and Broth</u>. They contain no fat and are marketed nationally by Homestat Farm, Ltd.

Interestingly, this product was available in the 1930's and even used by the Barron House on occasion when stringencies of time made that a good idea! Which brings me to Rule 3.

3. *Do your best to try G. Washington, but if you prefer another bouillon, use it. GW Brown is like beef bouillon and GW Golden is like chicken bouillon.*

As you cook soups, you will be tempted to improvise. Don't be shy. The worst that can happen is one not so great batch.

One of the best ways to ensure that leftovers are not wasted is to incorporate them into a new soup. In the Barron House kitchen, soups were a key means for avoiding waste that can be endemic when the partaking clientele can vary substantially in numbers. Hence Rule 4.

4. Don't be afraid to alter these soup recipes. But always do it to taste. And do try new combinations. They can be big winners.

Remember, soup-making is an art. Improvisation creates new artistic master-pieces. I wonder sometimes where the Barron House ever got the idea to put chili powder in asparagus soup...but it did!

A FEW ABBREVIATIONS I WILL USE

TBSP - tablespoon

tsp - teaspoon

G. Wash. Brown Broth - G. Washington Rich Brown Seasoning and Broth (1 packet equals enough for one cup of water). When substituting another bouillon or canned bouillon use 8 oz.

G. Wash. Golden Broth - G. Washington Golden Seasoning and Broth (1 packet equals enough for one cup of water). Substitute similarly here.

ABOUT ASPARAGUS

The first recipe is entitled INSPIRING ASPARAGUS SOUP. It was a favorite one at the Barron House, but unfortunately very seasonal because the hotel's asparagus patch had a very short period of production each year.

The wife of the Bohemian proprietor had a particularly loving feeling about this soup. She always claimed that it was asparagus that brought her to America. When she and her husband were thinking seriously about emigrating to America they elected a prudent approach. Her husband and his brother sailed to America without their families to see whether such a move would be wise. Could they find work? Could they get by without knowing English? Would Americans accept them?

When they arrived they set out across the American states looking for a place where their silk-weaving skills would be welcomed and where they might risk bringing their families. Work in the Chicago stockyards was not satisfactory. They took odd jobs to help defray their expenses as they looked. One of these jobs was harvesting asparagus.

The arrangement was that they were to cut the stalks with knives, put them in bushel baskets and be paid according to the number of bushels they filled. The two brothers worked hard. At the end of the first day they ached from bending and cutting, and their pay was meager. As the second morning progressed their assigned patches brought them near a shed. They noticed a scythe leaning against the shed. There were no bosses around, just the two brothers. "Why don't we try cutting with the scythe?" one asked the other, "That will go a lot faster."

In Bohemia all men grew up cutting hay and grass and grain with a scythe. There were no harvesting machines. The two brothers employed the Bohemian method, one cutting and the other filling bushels. By the end of the day they had a prodigious number of filled bushels. When the foreman came to check their production he was aghast.

John Bohumil

Though hampered by the language problem, it was obvious to the two brothers that their boss was upset. He managed to make them understand that he saw no way the two could have filled so many bushels and that he thought they must have stolen them from the other workers. The other pickers apparently convinced the foreman that none of their bushels were taken.

Finally the two brothers decided to try to explain by showing. They got the scythe and went to an unharvested patch. They cut asparagus and filled bushels. The foreman just stood there speechless for the longest time. The two brothers worried.

Then the foreman walked up to them and said, "You come back tomorrow. See me." The two brothers understood those words and worried what would happen to them the next day. After a sleepless night, they arrived early at the asparagus farm. The foreman was already there. Beside him, leaning against a building, were six scythes. He promoted the two brothers to straw bosses and had them teach and supervise the other workers, harvesting by scythe!

The future proprietor of the Barron House wrote to his wife in Bohemia to tell her that America was the right place for them. "In America," he wrote, "you don't need to be nobility or even to speak English well. You are rewarded for good work."

The two brothers brought their families to America.

INSPIRING ASPARAGUS SOUP

1. **BREAK OFF** and discard tough bottom end of each stalk for 1 **lb.** of fresh **asparagus**

> *This was standard operating procedure in the Barron House kitchen. You hold just below the tip on one end of the stalk and at the end on the other end. Then you bend until the stalk breaks naturally.*

2. **CUT OFF** and set aside the asparagus tips for use later.

3. **COOK** remaining pieces cut in one inch lengths in microwave on high with 1/4 **cup water** for 10 minutes until tender.

4. **BLEND TOGETHER** to a smooth thick liquid

~ the cooked asparagus pieces

~ 2 **TBSP shallots (or onion)** chopped

~ 2 **TBSP celery** chopped

~ 1/2 **tsp lemon juice**

~ 1 **TBSP light butter** or **margarine**

~ 1/2 **can undiluted low-fat cream of mushroom soup** (or regular)

~ 1/2 **tsp chili powder**

~ 2 **packets G. Wash. Brown Broth**

(You can substitute other bouillon cubes but that will alter taste a little)

5. **COOK** saved tips 3 minutes in microwave on high in 1/4 **cup water**

1. MIX TOGETHER AND HEAT just to boiling

~ blended liquid

~ asparagus tips and their water

~ 3/4 **cup skimmed milk**

~ 1/4 **cup dry non-dairy cream**

The Barron House Soups

BACON AND EGG DROP SOUP

This was a very Bohemian soup where meat was used sparingly but well.

1. **COOK** just to boiling

    ~2 1/2 **cups water**

    ~3 **G. Wash. Brown Broth** or 1 - 10 2 oz. can of beef broth and 1 cup water

    ~1 **cup skim milk**

    ~1/4 **cup dry non-dairy creamer**

2. **BEAT** 2 **egg beaters** and combine with

    ~5 **TBSP flour** (Wondra or regular)

    ~3 crumbled crisp pieces of lean **bacon**

3. Start broth **BOILING** gently

4. **POUR** egg mixture into hot broth while stirring broth

5. **ADD** salt, only if needed

There is bacon in this recipe. However, look for very lean bacon. Get it very crisp in the microwave. If you're still concerned, reduce to 2 slices, or 1.

John Bohumil

"BEAN AND OTHER" SOUP

At the Barron House this was really a "leftover" soup but the patrons did not know this. The men liked full-bodied soups and kept asking for this one. At times the House had to "manufacture" leftovers! This recipe assumes no leftovers but feel free to use them if you have any.

1. **COOK** over medium heat in 4 **TBSP Olive Oil** for 10 minutes

    ~ 2 small chopped **red onions**

    ~ 8 chopped medium **carrots**

    ~ 1 1/2 **cups** diced **celery** with leaves

    ~ 3 cloves minced **garlic**

2 **ADD, BRING TO A BOIL, AND SIMMER** for 15 minutes

    ~ 2 **quarts water**

    ~ 4 packets **G. Wash. Golden Broth**

    (You can substitute other chicken bouillon cubes but it will alter the taste)

    ~ 2 **cups** chopped **cabbage**

    ~ 1 **40 oz.** can of **northern beans**

    ~ 1/2 **tsp salt**

    ~ 1/2 **tsp pepper**

3. **ADD AND SIMMER** 30 minutes

    ~ 3 **cups** finely diced **potatoes**

    ~ 2 **cups** chopped fresh or frozen **spinach**

    (This can be added during the last 15 minutes)

The Barron House Soups

BODACIOUS BROCCOLI SOUP

This was one of the banquet soups. It looked elegant and was not filling when served in a cup. It was rarely served to the 21-meal men because they turned the "all the refills you want" rule into 4 or 5 servings. Available pots couldn't handle that volume, to say nothing of kitchen range space.

1. **COOK** in 2 **quarts** of **water** until tender

   ~ 3 **cups broccoli flowerlets** (absolutely NO STEMS)

2. **ADD AND COOK** for 6 minutes more

   ~ 3/4 **cup skim milk**

   ~1/4 **cup dry non-dairy creamer**

   (The Barron House used 1/2 cup heavy cream and a half cup water. You can, too, for a treat)

   ~ 4 **packets G. Wash. Golden Broth**

   ~ 2 **TBSP cornstarch** in a **half cup** of **cold water** to thicken

   (Use more if needed)

   ~ **salt** to taste

3. **CHOP** broccoli flowerlets just enough to make green bits

(Can be done by putting the soup in a blender for a few seconds. Of course you can do it the way it was done at the Barron House with a metal chopper in a wooden bowl. The blender is easier. I know.)

BROWN SOUP

In the Czech language this was called HRUBA POLIVKA (pronounced "hrew -bah poe leave kah") The regulars at the Barron House had a less dignified name for it. However, it was tantalizingly tasty on a cold night ... and very, very easy to make! To add to your worldly knowledge, browning flour this way can be described by you as "DELAM JISKU PRO POLIVKU" (pronounced "Dyellahm shees koo prough poe leave koo").

1. **MELT** 3 **TBSP light butter** or **margarine**

2. **ADD** 3 **TBSP Wondra flour** slowly and stir into paste

3. **HEAT** while stirring for a minute or two

4. **ADD**

    ~1 **can (10 1/2 oz) beef broth** or **consommé**

    ~1 **can water**

5. **BRING TO BOIL**

6. **REDUCE HEAT** to very low and heat 15 minutes or longer

BEEF BROTH SOUPS

In the Barron House kitchen a standing policy, which grew out of the Bohemian culture, was that nothing wholesome should be wasted. The kitchen was a prolific producer of a potato by-product, potato water. Potatoes were a year-round staple. They stored relatively well and provided a very desirable diet item. Most potatoes in those days were prepared by cooking in water. So the kitchen produced gallons of potato water each year. The Barron House did not waste potato water. As a result, the beef broth soups at the Barron House were really beef stock combined with potato water. The beef broth recipes below all use this beef stock potato water combination as their base.

THE COMBINED STOCK was made by heating together

~ 2 **quarts** of **potato water**

~ 4 **packets** of **G. Wash. Brown Broth**

BEEF WITH RICE AND POTATOES SOUP

COOK together until potatoes are fork tender and rice is soft

~ 2 **quarts** of **combined stock**

~ 2 large **potatoes** cut into small cubes

~ 1/2 **cup Minute Rice**

~ 2 **TBSP** chopped fresh **parsley**

BEEF WITH BARLEY SOUP

COOK together until barley is expanded and soft

~ 2 **quarts combined stock**

~ 3/4 **cup barley**

BEEF WITH CREAM OF WHEAT SOUP

COOK together for 10 minutes or more

~ 2 **quarts combined stock**

~ 3/4 **cup Cream of Wheat**

(or 4 instant single helping breakfast packets)

BEEF WITH EGG DROP SOUP

1. **BEAT** together

~ 2 whole **eggs**

~ 1/2 to 3/4 **cup flour**

(experiment with the amount to get the consistency you like best)

~ 1/4 **tsp** or so of **salt**

2. **BOIL** 2 **quarts** of **combined stock** and **DRIBBLE** egg mixture into boiling soup from a spoon

3. **MIX** soup quickly with a whisk to create pea-size or smaller egg drops

4. **HEAT** 5 minutes and **ADD**

~ 2 **TBSP** chopped fresh **parsley**

STALE BREAD BEEF SOUP

This was one of the "use it, don't waste it" soups. It was always clear that the baked bread had outstripped the need for bread when the big silver soup tureen appeared on a kitchen table. On the flat top of the big wood/coal stove a large pot of beef broth potato water would be heating along with several bricks. At mealtime the tureen would move to the dining room and be placed on two of the hot bricks. The servers in their starched white aprons, would take turns serving the soup. This was necessary because the stale bread beef soup (never called stale in front of the diners) would inevitably result in requests for thirds and fourths!

1. **COOK** to boiling

    ~ 2 **quarts combined beef broth potato water**

    ~ 1/2 **tsp pepper**

2. **SERVE** in soup bowl covering one whole slice of **bread**

John Bohumil

BOHEMIAN ALPHABET SOUP

After WWI, Bohemia became Czechoslovakia. The language of Bohemia was Czech. One of the soups the Barron House made from beef broth potato water stock was alphabet soup. If the House had a new worker he would be assigned to a big tray on a table in the kitchen removing all the "y's" from the alphabet macaroni for the soup. That was because he was told that for the soup to be authentically Bohemian it could not have any "y's" in it because the Czech alphabet does not have a "y". The truth is, it does, but only as a vowel not as a consonant. If the worker missed any, someone would remark, "Oh, it must have been a vowel" which, of course, left the new worker even further bewildered!

1. **COOK** to boil and **SIMMER** until the alphabet macaroni is soft.

~ 2 **quarts combined beef broth** and **potato water**

~ 1 **cup** of **alphabet macaroni** (with "y's" removed!)

CREDIBLE CAULI-BROC SOUP

The Barron House blended the two vegetables. Now there is a cross between these two vegetables that combines them.

1. **COOK** to boiling, and then **SIMMER** for 15 minutes

    ~ 3 **cups** chopped **broccoli** flowerlets

    ~ 3 **cups** chopped **cauliflower** flowerlets

    (or 6 cups of the combined vegetable)

    ~ 1 medium **onion** chopped

    ~ 2 **TBSP lemon juice**

    ~ 4 **cups skim milk**

    ~ 3/4 **cup dry non-dairy cream**

    ~ 2 **packets G. Wash. Golden Broth**

    (or 3 cubes chicken flavored bouillon)

    ~ 3/4 **tsp salt**

    ~ 2 **TBSP butter**

    ~ 2 **TBSP flour**

2. **BLEND** to liquid in blender

John Bohumil

CLASSY CABBAGE SOUP

This was always called CABBAGE soup at the Barron House because the bulk of the clientele would have questioned making soup out of brussel sprouts. The Barron House cooks liked using them because they stayed available even after the frosts and snow came. I have to agree, BRUSSEL SPROUT SOUP would sound strange!

1. HEAT in 1 **TBSP butter** and **1 TBSP margarine** until soft

~ 1/2 cup finely chopped **onion** (white or yellow)

~ 8 finely chopped **brussel sprouts**

2. ADD, BRING TO A BOIL, then **SIMMER** for 15 minutes

~ 1 **quart water**

~ 3 **packets** of **G. Wash. Brown Broth**

(You can substitute other beef bouillon cubes but it will alter the taste)

3. SERVE with a glob of **sour cream** mixed with chopped **parsley** and **caraway seeds**

The Barron House Soups

NON-FAT CHICKEN NOODLE SOUP

This soup was normally made with chicken broth and homemade noodles. However, sometimes the chicken stock was depleted and the cooks would resort to using 'good old G. Washington Golden". The recipe I'm providing uses G. W. not chicken stock. The cooks would roll out the egg noodle dough on a 2 by 4 foot bread board and let me cut the noodles with a do-hickey that had a bunch of sharp wheels. One helper got inventive and overlapped the cuts so the noodles were 1/8 inch wide instead of 3/8 inch wide. He was duly censored with "chicken soup is not chicken soup without wide noodles". I must admit I didn't like chicken soup don't, except this one, which, thankfully for me, doesn't have chicken in it and it's a lot better for it!

1. **SIMMER 5 cups** of **water** for 10 minutes after bringing to a boil with

> ~ 3 **packets** of **G. Wash. Golden Broth**
>
> (or if you like chicken you may use 3 chicken bouillon cubes)
>
> ~ 2 **TBSP** chopped **fresh parsley**
>
> ~ **8 oz** of **WIDE egg noodles**

The large clothing factory down the street from the Barron House was owned and run by Nat Warsaw. Nat was Jewish and would eat occasionally at the Barron House. His finest remark (I felt) was the day he had a bowl of this "chicken" soup and remarked, "You know it's better than my Mother made!" That was a G. W. Golden day! He never knew his chicken soup had no chicken.

John Bohumil

CAPTIVATING CARROT SOUP

Fresh carrots store pretty well so this soup was a regular for months in the summer and fall. Today they're available year round and pretty inexpensive, a nice soupcon of saving for your budget.

1. **HEAT** until soft in 2 **TBSP margarine** or **light butter.**

    ~ 1 chopped medium **onion**

    ~ 3 minced cloves of **garlic** (omit if you're not fond of garlic)

    ~ 1 **tsp thyme**

    ~ 1 **bay leaf**

2. **ADD** and **BRING TO A BOIL**, then **SIMMER** 30 minutes.

    ~ 6 **cups** peeled and thin-sliced **carrots**

    ~ 2 **cups** peeled diced **potatoes**

    ~ 4 **packets G. Wash. Golden Broth**

    (or 4 other chicken bouillon cubes)

    ~ Enough **water** to fully cover vegetables, plus 2 cups

3. **PUREE** until smooth (after removing bay leaf)

Ricing carrots even when they're nicely soft was a tiresome chore. Like having an electric starter to replace cranking on automobiles, it's nice to be able to puree in a blender.

CHARD AND CARROT SOUP

Swiss chard was not Bohemian but it grows profusely so the Barron House saw it as a "money crop". If you raise chard, this is a great way to use it and the result is freezable for year round use.

1. **HEAT** in 2 **TBSP olive oil** and 2 **TBSP light butter** until onion is soft.

    ~ 1 minced clove of **garlic**

    ~ 1/4 **cup** chopped **onion**

    ~ 1 medium peeled and grated **carrot**

2. **MICROWAVE** on high for 5 minutes

    ~ 3/4 **cup** diced **potato**

    ~ 1 **cup water**

    ~ 2 **G. Wash. Golden Broth**

3. **COMBINE** 1 and 2 above, **ADD**, and **SIMMER** until chard is fully wilted

    ~ 2 **qts** chopped fresh **chard**

    ~ 2 **cups water**

    ~ 2 more **G. Wash. Golden Broth**

4. **BLEND** to liquid and **ADD**

    ~ 2 **cups skim milk**

    ~ 1/4 **cup dry non-fat creamer**

    ~ **Pepper** and **salt** to taste

5. **HEAT** for serving

CELERY-SPINACH CREAM SOUP

1. **HEAT** in 3 **TBSP light butter** until soft

    ~ 1/4 **cup** chopped **shallot** (or onion)

2. **COOK** 3 minutes on high in microwave in 1/2 cup **water**

    ~ 1 **cup** chopped **celery**

    ~ 1 1/2 **cups** chopped **fresh spinach** with stems

3. **COOK** 1 and 2 above together at boiling for 2 minutes with

    ~ 2 **cups skim milk**

    ~ 1/4 **cup dry non-dairy cream**

    ~ 1 **cup water**

    ~ 3 **packets G. Wash. Golden Broth**

4. **TAKE OUT** all spinach and 1/2 of the celery and puree them to liquid

5. **RETURN** to pot and **SIMMER** 10 minutes with

    ~ 1 1/2 **tsp corn starch** in 1/2 **cup cold water**

6. **SPRINKLE** with 2 **TBSP** chopped **fresh parsley**

Finished soup should have spinach fully liquefied with half the celery. The other half of the celery will be in small pieces. The combination provides a distinctive taste. This was the way the Barron House "handled" the diners who claimed to dislike spinach soup or celery soup, etc. The combination soup put them in a quandary, and they just ate it!

CHEESE AND ONION SOUP

Bohemians liked cheese and this soup has the onion as an "adder".

1. **HEAT** in 1 **TBSP olive oil** and 2 **TBSP vegetable oil** until lightly browned.

    ~ 1 **cup** of **onion** cut in half and sliced thin

2. **ADD** and **SIMMER** until potatoes are fully cooked

    ~ 5 **cups water**

    ~ 2 **packets G. Wash. Brown Broth**

    ~ 1 **packet G. Wash. Golden Broth**

    ~ 3/4 **cup** of **grated potato**

3. **ADD** and **HEAT** until cheese is melted

    ~ 2 **cups** grated **extra sharp** or **sharp cheddar**

    (low fat, if available)

    ~ 1 **cup skim milk**

    ~ 1 **tsp soy sauce**

COOL CUCUMBER SOUP

Cucumbers grew well in Bohemia and even better in Pennsylvania. Cucumbers appeared on the Barron House table in salads, in sour cream, and in soups. This particular soup was very popular with the working crews. Sometimes it was served hot and sometimes it was served cold, but always with a large dab of sour cream (except for Charlie Lee, the British merchant seaman, who became landlocked at the Barron House - he took it with a slice of lemon.)

The recipe as I present it makes a large quantity. The soup freezes well but if you want a smaller batch, adjust all ingredients down.

1. **HEAT** in 4 **TBSP vegetable oil** until soft

    ~ 1 **cup** of chopped **red onion**

2. **COOK** by bringing to a boil and **SIMMERING** for 30 to 45 minutes

    ~ the onion above

    ~ 6 large **unpeeled cucumbers** cut in chunks

    ~ 10 **cups** of **water**

    ~ 6 **packets G. Wash. Brown Broth** (or 10 beef flavor bouillon cubes)

    ~ 4 tsp **vinegar** (any kind)

    ~ 6 **TBSP** instant **Cream of Wheat**

    ~ 1/2 **tsp dill seed**

    ~ **salt** to taste

3. **PUREE** in blender until all cucumber seeds and pulp are liquefied

When the Barron House made this soup the cucumbers were peeled and seeded. This is one soup where the new recipe is better!

John Bohumil

CUCUMBER CREAM SOUP

This was another banquet soup at the Barron House. However, when it was made, enough was always saved for Charlie Lee's dinner. On the days this soup was made it was all he ate.

1. **BLEND** thoroughly in a blender

    ~ 5 **cups** peeled and seeded **cucumbers**

    ~ 1/2 **cup** chopped **onion**

    (The Barron House couldn't, but use **Vidalia** onion if you can)

    ~ 1 clove **garlic**

    ~ 2 **cups water**

    ~ 2 **packets G. Wash. Golden Broth**

    (or 3 chicken flavored bouillon cubes)

2. **MIX** with

    ~ 2 **cups low fat sour cream**

    (or real sour cream, if you dare)

    ~ 1 1/2 **cups skim milk**

    ~ 3 **TBSP wine vinegar**

    ~ **salt** to taste

3. **CHILL** and serve with

    ~ chopped **fresh chives** on top

    (or with **chives and** chopped **tomatoes** dropped on top - my preference)

CURRY WATER SOUP

This was a soup for leftovers, i.e. meat and vegetables. A good mix was with leftover ham. Lamb would probably also work.

1. **BROWN** in 3 **TBSP vegetable oil**

    ~ 1 **cup** small cubes of leftover **ham**

    ~ 1/4 **cup** chopped **onion**

2. **ADD, BRING TO A BOIL** and **SIMMER** until vegetables are tender

    ~ 5 **cups water**

    ~ 1 **16 oz can pinto beans**

    ~ 1 **packet G. Wash. Golden Broth**

    ~ 1/4 **tsp pepper**

    ~ 1 **TBSP mild curry** (or more)

    ~ 1 **cup vegetables** cut in tiny pieces with a vegetable chopper. Any mild vegetables, leftover, cooked, or raw will do, such as: carrots, broccoli, corn, celery, green beans, peas, tomato, etc.

    ~ **salt** to taste

This is an amazingly good soup. Keep the vegetables sparse. Soup should be thin, predominantly liquid. Curries vary in taste so use your discretion and add more or less, to your taste. Add water, too, if needed.

GRACIOUS GREEN HAM SOUP

This soup was made at the Barron House by using a massive hand grinder. I still have one and when fully equipped with a variety of "insides" you can grind almost anything. However, I recommend doing the "grinding" with your tried and true blender.

1. **HEAT 1/2 package** of **French cut green beans** in your microwave until soft

2. **ADD**

    ~ 1/2 **cup** thin-sliced **ham** which you have chopped into small pieces (Do your best to buy no water, or 3% water or less ham)

    ~1 **cup sharp cheddar** chunks

    ~ 4 **cups water**

    ~ 8 **oz skim milk**

    ~ 1/4 **cup dry non-dairy creamer** (or substitute 8 oz cream for milk and dry cream presuming your last cholesterol broke under 175)

3. **CHOP** in blender until mix has only tiny or no pieces of anything

4. **ADD**

    ~ 1/4 **tsp nutmeg** (no more!)

    ~ 2 **TBSP light butter**

    ~ 2 **G. Wash Golden Broth**

    ~ 2 **TBSP corn starch**

5. **HEAT** and **EAT**

GLORIOUS GREEN PEA SOUP

This is not a renowned soup, but it should be. And it is so simple to make. If you try it, I'd bet my waistcoat you'll like it!

1. **COOK** until hot after mixing thoroughly

    ~ 1 **can** Campbell's **Green Pea Soup** (condensed 10 1/2 oz or 11 1/4 oz)

    ~ 2 soup **cans** of **water**

    ~ 1 **packet** of **G. Wash. Brown Broth**

    MAKE NO SUBSTITUTIONS

John Bohumil

GYPSY SOUP

Bohemia was an advanced culture and it was located in a part of Europe where many advancing cultures lived side by side. To some people the term gypsy connotes undesirable traits. However, the word itself comes from a belief that the people had originated in Egypt. Another view ties them to India and their language to a Northwestern Indian dialect.

This soup originated with the Barron House proprietor's wife from a friend in her village in Bohemia, a woman who had come from the near-Eastern melting pot area. Unfortunately, the recipe was only partially written down. And it is quite certain that the original recipe did not contain tomatoes. I remember it by taste.

What happened to me is that an old friend of ours shared a recipe with us that tastes almost exactly like what I remember. She lives now in a Washington, D. C. suburb and her name is Pat Reynolds. She does not claim lineage to the Near East, but her soup could! (Except for the tomatoes, of course!)

1. **FRY** lightly in 3 **TBSP olive oil** until the onion is soft

    ~ a chopped good-sized **Spanish onion** (not Near East!)

    ~ a chopped large **green pepper**

    ~ 1 **TBSP minced garlic**

2. **ADD** 1 **lb** of very lean **ground beef** and continue to fry until meat is no longer pink

3. **ADD** to meat mix and stir in

    ~ 2 **TBSP chili powder**

    ~ 1 **TBSP cumin**

    ~ 1 **TBSP coriander**

~ 3 **TBSP chopped parsley** (fresh or dry)

4. **ADD**

~ 4 **cups water** and

> **OR** 3 10 1/2 oz cans chicken broth

~ 4 **G. Wash. Golden Broth**

~ 16 **oz** of **diced canned tomatoes** with juice

~ 16 **oz** to 28 oz of **red kidney beans** (to taste)

~ 3 **cups** thinly sliced **carrots** cooked to soft in your microwave

~ 1 **cup** dry **rice** microwaved to full cooked state

4. **SIMMER** 20 to 30 minutes

5. **ADD salt** if needed and **black pepper**

I remember the proprietor's wife talking about adding leftovers to the CIKANSKY POLEVKA and the proprietor always shaking his head, "No." Then he would add what he had learned as a new American, "We don't put egg in our beer."

John Bohumil

LUMINOUS LETTUCE SOUP

Even for good gardeners lettuce can become overabundant. It never did at the Barron House. The excess could always end up as a very tasty soup.

1. **COOK** in covered pan for 5 minutes

    ~ 1 **lb.** of **leaf lettuce**

    ~ **water** enough to prevent burning

2. **COOK** in another pot in 2 **TBSP light butter** or **margarine**

    ~ 2 **TBSP** chopped **onion**

3. **STIR** into 2 above

    ~ 2 **TBSP flour**

    ~ 2 **cups skim milk**

    ~ 2 **cups water**

    ~ 3 (or 4) **packets** of **G. Wash. Brown Broth**

    (or 4 beef flavored bouillon cubes)

    ~ 3 **TBSP Cream of Wheat**

4. **ADD, BRING TO BOIL,** and **SIMMER** until soup thickens

    ~ the cooked lettuce

5. **CHOP** in blender at high speed until everything liquefies

6. **ADD salt** (if needed) to taste

LUSTROUS LEEK SOUP

1. **COOK** until soft in 2 **TBSP butter** or **margarine**

    ~ 2 **cup** chopped **onion**

    ~ 1 chopped **shallot**

2. **ADD, BRING TO A BOIL**, and **SIMMER** until potatoes fork tender

    ~ 1/2 **cup** finely chopped peeled **carrot**

    ~ 1/4 **cup** finely chopped **celery**

    ~ 1/2 **cup** chopped **tomatoes** (fresh or canned)

    ~ 1 **TBSP soy sauce**

    ~ 1 **tsp lemon juice**

    ~ 3 **packets** of **G. Wash. Golden Broth**

    (or 4 cubes chicken flavored bouillon)

    · 3 cups water

    ~ 2 **cups** chopped **potatoes**

    ~ 2 chopped **leeks**

    ~ 2 **tsp chives**

    ~ 1/4 **tsp cayenne**

    ~ **salt** to taste

3. **BLEND** in blender until soupy

John Bohumil

MARBLE SOUP

1. **MICROWAVE** until soft

    ~ 1/4 **cup** of **turnips** cut into small thin pieces

    ~ 1/2 **cup celery** chopped into very small pieces

2. **ADD** to the above vegetables and **SIMMER** for 10 minutes

    ~ 1 **cup tomato puree** or **crushed tomatoes**

    ~ 3 **cups water**

    ~ 1 **cup G. Wash. Brown Broth** or 1 cup beef bouillon

3. **MIX** together

    ~ 1/4 **lb ground lean beef**

    ~ 1/2 **tsp onion salt**

    ~ 1/4 **tsp garlic powder**

    ~ 1 beaten **egg**

    ~ 1 **packet G. Wash Brown Broth**

    ~ 2 **tsp paprika**

4. **ROLL** meat mixture out like a candle and cut at 1/2 inch intervals to make tiny meat balls.

5. **FRY** meat balls until no longer pink in **olive oil** or **vegetable oil**

6. **ADD** meatballs to tomato/vegetable mixture and simmer for 5 minutes

---

At the Barron House this soup was commonly made when the tomato harvest got out of hand. Fresh tomatoes were used in lieu of the puree and can be by you, too

---

The Barron House Soups

MANIFOLD MATZO SOUP

Nat Warsaw, the factory owner down the street, dropped any number of hints that the "kitchen" as he called it should be able to make the Jewish delicacy, Matzo Ball soup. One day he brought in a recipe. The cooks obligingly made up a batch but the proprietor's wife wouldn't serve it. "Neni pravy" she insisted, "It's not right."

Bohemia was quite cosmopolitan in some ways and certainly had its variety of religions. There were Roman Catholics, Lutherans and John Hus' Hussites, Jews, followers of Islam, etc. It seemed she had an "old country" friend of Jewish background and had eaten her Matzo Ball soup, or so she thought. And it was not like Nat's.

As I suggested to you in my introductory comments, experimentation is good. The Matzo soup recipe here is not Nat Warsaw's. But it is excellent and the way the "Neni pravy" cook remembered her friend's soup (except for the tomato sauce which the cook added to "Americanize" it for the regular clientele).

Unless your family heritage puts you in the category of being able to make the best matzo balls west of Israel, make it easy on yourself:

1. **BUY** and **PREPARE** a Matzo-ball mix according to the instructions on the package. Use real eggs and refrigerate dough 15 minutes.

2. **HOWEVER,** make the Matzo balls as small as you can (marbles or smaller)

3. **DROP INTO** 2 1/2 **quarts** of boiling salted **water, COVER,** and **SIMMER** for 20 minutes on lower heat (this assumes a dry mix of a 2 1/2 oz size)

4. **COOK** in microwave until soft

    ~ 1/4 **cup** finely chopped **celery**

~ 1/2 **cup** finely chopped **carrot**

~ 2 finely chopped **green scallions** or 2 **TBSP onion**

5. COMBINE AND HEAT TOGETHER

~ the strained Matzo balls

~ the vegetables

~ **4 oz tomato sauce**

~ **7 cups G. Wash. Golden Broth** (or 7 cups chicken bouillon)

The Barron House Soups

MEAGER MEAT SOUP

The Pennsylvania Dutch and the early settlers of New England all had versions of meat soup. Most, however, would never do in a heart friendly cookbook.

As luck would have it, the Barron House cooks had developed a special meat soup for emergencies. The idea was that you could produce it with little work and very simple ingredients (which they almost always had available or could get quickly form the local butcher shop!)

Also, as you will see, it cooks itself. Best of all, it is very, very low on fat, especially with today's pork.

1. **REMOVE** every scrap of fat (and the bone if there is one) from 2 pork chops

(Frozen are fine, just defrost first).

2. **BROWN** on both sides well in olive oil.

3. **PUT IN OVEN - SAFE DISH** with:

~ **5 cups of water** and

~ **3 G. Wash Golden Broth** or 2 cups water and 3 cups of chicken broth

4. **COVER AND BAKE** at 350 degrees for 1 1/2 hours (or until pork is tender enough to flake.

5. **CHOP** up pork until it looks like hamburger and add:

~ **1 tsp marjoram leaves**

~ **1 tsp basil leaves**

6. **SEASON** with a little salt, if needed.

John Bohumil

For your Czech vocabulary (colloquial):

To je masova polivka

(This is meat soup)

.

The Barron House Soups

MISTER T'S WHITE CRAB SOUP

Mr. Trexler (or Mister T. as all the regulars called him) had his bedroom and office on the third floor of the Barron House. He was its longest and most sophisticated tenant.

He took all his meals at the House (as he called it).

He was very punctual and always entered the dining room at exactly 6 P. M. for his dinner. However, except during Prohibition, his dinner always started with a Manhattan. I can't remember the whiskey used but I know it was the best the House had. His Manhattan had to be made with shaved ice in a silver shaker and served in the V-shaped crystal stem glass which was his alone.

Mr. Trexler was a professional insurance agent and arrived at dinner in a white shirt, tie and suit every season of the year. As you could guess, there was a Mr. T's chair in the dining room. No one else dared to sit in it.

The other diners always knew when White Crab Soup was being served at dinner because Mr. T's Manhattan was delivered <u>with</u> the silver shaker. He always had <u>two</u> Manhattans on White Crab Soup night.

The regulars never started their meals on White Crab Soup night until he had finished both Manhattans. As a favor to them, he would lightly tap his glass with a spoon to indicate he had.

I have never been able to determine whether Mr. T. had <u>two</u> Manhattans because he liked the White Crab Soup or because he needed two to be able to eat it.

1. **FRY** in 2 **TBSP light butter or margarine** until the onion is soft

~ 1/4 **cup** finely chopped <u>white</u> **onion**

~ 1/4 **cup** finely chopped heart of the **celery**

~ 3 **TBSP** chopped fresh traditional **parsley**

2. **ADD** 6 **oz** of finely chopped **crab meat**. If using canned, use only high quality.

3. **MIX** and **HEAT** for two to three minutes

4. **ADD**

~ 1 1/2 **pints skim milk**

~ 1/2 **cup dry non-dairy creamer**

~ 1/4 **cup** good quality dry **sherry**

5. **HEAT** just to boiling and simmer 6 to 8 minutes.

The Barron House Soups

MINI-MUSHROOM SOUP

1. **COOK** in 6 **TBSP butter** or **light butter** lightly

    ~ 10 **oz mushrooms** chopped in small bits

    ~ 6 **oz mushrooms** cut in slices

2. **COOK, BRING TO BOIL** and **SIMMER** about 10 minutes

    ~ the mushrooms from 1 above

    ~ 8 **TBSP flour**

    ~ 4 **TBSP** chopped **shallots** (or onion)

    ~ 1/4 **cup** finely chopped **celery**

    ~ 2 **TBSP** chopped fresh **parsley**

    ~ 3 **packets** of **G. Wash. Brown Broth**

    (or 4 beef flavored bouillon cubes)

    ~ 3 cups water

3. **ADD** 1/4 **cup sherry** or **port wine**, **MIX** and serve

---

The Pennsylvania Dutch, the Czechs, and the Slovaks were all big on growing and/or hunting mushrooms. I was always glad that the Barron House stuck with buying commercially available ones. Two of my acquaintances, who considered themselves experts, died of mushrooms they picked.

I can't categorize this soup by culture. But before and after Prohibition it was a Barron House favorite.

Don't short cut. The ten ounces <u>must</u> be chopped into small bits or the wine cannot do its job.

John Bohumil

NUSSBAUM'S GONE FISHING SOUP

Harry Nussbaum was the butcher at the American Store. Even though the town had just a smattering of Roman Catholic and Jewish families Harry had fresh fish for sale every Friday and his own gefullete fisch salted trout and fish stock that he prepared Thursday and sold Friday.

He liked to eat at the Barron House and managed to talk the cooks into making soup out of the trout. The regular diners always recognized Harry's soup and named it after him.

This recipe is Harry's. However, I recommend buying a jar of gefilter fish to short cut its preparation. Of course, if you're a purist, feel free to make you own, salting and grinding and mixing the fish filets from scratch and boiling your own broth from the fish skin and bones!

To Harry's credit, the non-Semitic crowd of eaters regularly went for seconds and thirds on his soup!

1. **COOK** in microwave until soft

    ~ 4 **TBSP** chopped **celery** with leaves

    ~ 4 **TBSP** chopped **carrots** (the small frozen ones sliced are perfect)

2. **ADD**

    ~ 1 **15 oz** jar of already prepared **gefilte fish** (cut into 1/2 inch squares) with the broth from the jar

    ~ 1 **8 or 10 oz** jar of **clam juice** (or your own fish broth, if you prefer)

    ~ 1 **cup water**

3. **HEAT** the above to boiling and **ADD**

    ~ 1 **cup G. Wash. Golden Broth** (or 1 cup chicken broth)

4. **KEEP BOILING** and **ADD SLOWLY**

～ 1 beaten **egg yolk** mixed with 3 **TBSP** of the boiling soup

John Bohumil

BOHEMIAN POTATO SOUP

In those Barron House days they ate lots of potatoes. But if you worked outdoors, hard work, those carbohydrates were nice to have.

1. **HEAT** in salted water to cover until the potatoes fork soft

    ~ 3 **cups** of peeled raw **potatoes** cut in small chunks

    ~ 1/4 **cup** of **onion** slices

2. **REMOVE** onion and discard, **MASH** drained potatoes leaving some small pieces

3. **SCALD**

    ~ 1 **quart skim milk**

4. **ADD** to scalded milk

    ~ 1/4 **cup dry non-dairy creamer**

    ~ 1 **tsp salt** (more if needed)

    ~ 1/4 **tsp pepper**

    ~ 1 **tsp celery salt**

    ~ 1 **TBSP** chopped **parsley**

    ~ 2 **TBSP flour** mixed with 4 **TBSP** melted **light butter**

    ~ large pinch of **cayenne**

5. **COMBINE** and add additional **salt** if needed

    ~ pureed potatoes from 2 above

    ~ scalded milk from 4 above

6. **HEAT** to boiling and serve with

    ~ **croutons** made by frying small bread squares in light butter

This was a soup which came from Bohemia. Cayenne, celery salt, and croutons were added here in America.

John Bohumil

PRETENTIOUS PUMPKIN SOUP

Pumpkins grow easily and this was a popular soup.

1. **HEAT** in 2 **TBSP vegetable oil**

    ~ 1 small chopped **onion**

2. **ADD** and **COOK** covered on medium heat 5 minutes

    ~ 2 **cups** peeled and diced **pumpkin** or canned

    ~ 3 **cups water**

    ~ 1 1/2 **cups** sliced (very thin) peeled **carrots**

    ~ 2 **cups potatoes** cut in chunks

    ~ 2 **TBSP lemon juice**

3. **ADD**, bring to **BOIL**, and **SIMMER** until potatoes fork easily

    ~ 2 **cups water**

    ~ 3 **packets G. Wash. Golden Broth** or 4 cubes chicken flavored bouillon

    ~ 1/2 **tsp basil**

4. **BLEND** in blender to liquid

RED CRAB SOUP

Bohemia was land-locked and ocean seafood was not a regular part of the population's diet. However, the Barron House served much seafood in the form of salads, patties, stews, etc. It is probably true that this part of the menu came via New England.

This soup was very popular.

1. **FRY** in 3 **TBSP light butter** or **margarine** until soft

    ~ 1/2 **cup** finely chopped **onion**

    ~ 1/4 **cup** finely chopped green or preferably **red pepper**

    ~ 1/4 **cup** finely chopped **celery**

    ~ 1 chopped small clove **garlic**

2. **ADD**

    ~ 3 **oz tomato paste**

    ~ 2 1/2 **cups water**

    ~ 1 **G. Wash. Brown Broth**

    ~ 1/4 **tsp basil**

    ~ 1/4 **tsp thyme**

    ~ 1/4 **tsp marjoram**

    ~ 6 **oz** chopped **crabmeat**

    ~ 4 **oz skim milk**

    ~ 1/4 **cup dry non-dairy creamer**

    ~ 1/2 **cup dry red wine**

3. **HEAT** to boiling, then **SIMMER** 6 to 8 minutes

RED CHOWDER

This will remind you of Manhattan Clam Chowder, but it isn't.

1. **MICROWAVE** to very crisp 2 thin slices of lean **bacon**

2. **FRY** 1/2 **cup** minced **onion** until soft in **light butter** or **margarine**

3. **MICROWAVE** until soft

 ~ 1/4 **cup** finely chopped **green pepper**

 ~ 1/4 **cup** finely chopped **celery**

 ~ 1/4 **cup** finely chopped **carrots**

 ~ 1/2 **cup** diced **potatoes**

4. **COMBINE** and **SIMMER** for 5 minutes

 ~ crumbled **bacon**

 ~ minced **onion**

 ~ microwaved **vegetables**

 ~ 5 **cups water**

 ~ 3 **cups clam juice**

 Or

 1 cup chopped canned clams and

 2 cups water

5. **ADD** and **SIMMER** for 8 to 10 minutes

 ~ 1 **cup** diced **tomatoes**

 ~ 1/3 **cup catsup**

 ~ 1 **tsp thyme**

- ~ 2 **TBSP** fresh **parsley** (or 1 TBSP dry)
- ~ 1 **tsp Worcestershire sauce**
- ~ 1 **bay leaf**
- ~ 1/4 **tsp ground cloves**

John Bohumil

SMOKY ONION SOUP

This was an unusual soup that was sometimes used for banquets but was also very popular with the work crews when the bread was still warm from baking - as the bread always was!

1. **COOK** in 3 **TBSP light butter** or **butter** until lightly browned

    ~ 1 medium **white onion** cut in half and sliced thinly

    ~ 1 large thinly sliced **shallot**

    (The Barron House could not always get shallots but you can, so do)

2. **ADD** and **SIMMER** until the potatoes are soft to the fork

    ~ 3/4 **cup** grated **potatoes**

    ~ **dash** of **soy sauce**

    ~ 4 **cups water**

    ~ 1 **cup skim milk**

    ~ 4 **TBSP dry non-dairy creamer**

    ~ 2 **packets G. Wash. Brown Broth** and 2 **Golden Broth**

    (or 3 beef flavored and 3 chicken flavored bouillon cubes)

3. **REDUCE HEAT** and **COOK** until cheese is melted and add **SALT** if needed

    ~ 1/2 **cup** grated **Velveeta** (low fat is fine)

    ~ 1 **cup** grated **sharp cheddar cheese** (low fat is fine)

    ~ 1/4 to 1 **cup** grated **smokey Gouda** or **smoke house cheese**, or **Smokey Swiss** (select amount based on taste)

    Because cheese varies in saltiness, adjust to taste by adding salt or more water.

The Barron House was able to get the smokey cheese and other appropriate cheeses from the American Store, a national grocery, just a half block away. We can't exactly duplicate what they bought but this combination is very, very close.

John Bohumil

SPINACH ESCAROLE SOUP

The Barron House grew and also bought from local farmers all types of fresh vegetables. Potatoes were bought by the ton and stored in a cold cellar. When they first arrived there were many new potato dishes.

Greens were a different story. They had to be used as available. So the variety of soups using greens was substantial. I have included only a few. This one has an especially attractive taste in my opinion. It sounds weird but try it. You may be pleasantly surprised.

1. **TEAR** into pieces (discarding thick stems) and cook in 2 **cups** of **water** 8 to 10 minutes

    ~ 1/2 of a **one lb. package** of **spinach**

    ~ 1/2 of a **one lb. package** of **escarole**

2. **FRY** in 8 TBSP **light butter or margarine** until soft

    ~ 5 **TBSP** chopped **scallions** or **onions**

3. **ADD** 6 TBSP **flour** and continue to heat 2 minutes

4. **ADD** to butter/flour mix

    ~ 2 **cups skim milk** and 1/2 **cup dry non-dairy creamer**

    ~ 4 **cups water**

    ~ 6 G. Wash. Golden Broth packet

5. **PUREE** cooked spinach and escarole with 1/2 cup of its water

6. **ADD** puree to butter flour mix

7. **BRING TO BOIL**, then **SIMMER** 6 to 8 minutes

8. **SERVE** with grated parmesan cheese

Seriously, isn't it surprisingly good?

SIMMERED SPLIT PEA SOUP

The Barron House made split pea soup using potato water and served it with croutons made with home-baked white bread.

1. **COOK** together, **BOILING** for 5 minutes and **LET STAND** for at least one hour

    ~ 10 **cups** of **potato water** (or if not available, just water)

    ~ 16 **oz** rinsed **split peas**

2. **COOK** at **SIMMER** for 3 hours, adding more water if soup gets sluggishly thick

    ~ the potato water pea mixture from 1 above

    ~ 1 **cup** chopped **celery** with leaves (use the tops of the stalks)

    ~ 3/4 **cup** chopped **onion** (including, if possible, 2 chopped **scallions** with their green stems)

    ~ 3/4 **cup** peeled **carrots** sliced thin, with each slice quartered to make small pieces

    ~ 1 large clove **garlic** split in half

    ~ 1/2 **tsp** thyme

3. **BLEND** in a blender or food processor to liquid most of the soup mixture, keeping out some of the carrots and whole split peas

4. **COOK** to boiling, **SIMMER** 10 minutes or so

    ~ blended soup and portion held out from 3 above

    ~ 1/2 to 1 **cup** (your taste) of small chunks of cooked **ham** with no fat (can be leftovers or a cut-up ham slice)

    ~ 2 **TBSP corn starch** in 1/2 **cup** cold **water**

    ~ **salt** to taste

5. **SERVE** with **butter croutons** (Freeze left-overs. This soup freezes well.)

To Make BUTTER CROUTONS

Cut squares of coarse white bread (like home-made) and fry in light butter on top and bottom. Make a lot!

SQUISHY SQUASH SOUP

When the squashes take over your garden this is the soup for you.

1. **HEAT** in a large pot in 4 **TBSP light butter**

    ~ 1/2 **cup** chopped **green onions**

    ~ 1/2 **cup** chopped **celery** with leaves

2. **COOK** to **BOILING**, then **SIMMER** 20 minutes

    ~ the onion and celery from 1 above

    ~ 2 **qts green** and **yellow young summer squash** unpeeled (older squash can be used if you take out the seeds) and cut in small pieces

    ~ 2 **cups water**

    ~ 4 **packets G. Wash. Golden Broth**

    (or 6 chicken flavored bouillon cubes)

    ~ 2 **cups skim milk**

    ~ 1/4 **cup dry non-dairy creamer**

    ~ 1 **tsp** chopped **chives**

    ~ **salt** to taste

    ~ 1/2 **tsp basil**

    ~ 1/2 **tsp oregano**

3. **PUREE** in blender and **SERVE ICE COLD** (with or without a dollop of sour cream)

SWISS CHARD SOUP

By now, if you've used a number of the recipes in this collection, I'm sure you've noted astutely that a number of the recipes follow a sort of pattern formula, i.e. butter, onion, celery, broth, milk, dry cream. You're right. Now think about the chard in your garden - maybe it should go the way of the squash and all those other prolific vegetables ... so ...

1. **COOK** in 2 **cups water** until floppy like cooked spinach

    ~ 12 **cups** loosely packed **Swiss chard** leaf parts (NO STEMS)

2. **COOK** in another pan in 2 **cups** of **water** until soft

    ~ 1/2 **cup** chopped **onion**

    ~ 1 **cup** chopped **celery** with leaves

3. **MIX** both of the above together with

    ~ 6 **packets** of **G. Wash. Golden Broth**

    (or 8 chicken flavored bouillon cubes)

4. **BLEND** at high speed to liquid

5. **COOK** the mixture to **BOILING** with

    ~ 4 **cups skim milk**

    ~ 1/2 **cup dry non-dairy creamer**

    ~ **salt** to taste

    ~ 2 **TBSP cornstarch** mixed in 1/4 cup **water**

The Barron House Soups

SURPRISING SAUSAGE SOUP

This was a cold weather winter soup that "regulars" at the Barron House liked to eat by dipping Italian or French bread into it. The days it was available bar customers (after Prohibition ended) often ordered it to have with their beer. It had been a favorite dish in Bohemia because it was robust, filling, and used very little meat. I recommend using the Jones Farm type of low fat with rice sausage links or no meat sausage links. Both preserve the original taste.

1. **MICROWAVE 4 slices** of preferably thick hickory smoked **bacon** until crisp and set aside

2. **HEAT** in a heavy iron pan in 3 **TBSP olive oil**

    ~ 1/2 **cup** peeled and chopped **carrots**

    ~ 1/4 **cup** chopped **red** and **green** fresh **pepper**

    ~ 1/2 **cup celery** chopped with leaves

    ~ 3/4 **cup** chopped white or yellow **onion**

3. **BROWN** in a separate pan

    ~ 6 **brown and serve breakfast link sausages** cut in 1/4 inch pieces

    (like Jones Farm low fat with rice links or no meat links)

4. **MIX** in the heavy iron pan with the carrots, pepper, celery, and onion in 2 above

    ~ the set aside bacon crumbled from 1 above

    ~ 5 **cups water**

    ~2 **cups fresh tomatoes** with skins, cut up in chunks (or of cut up canned tomatoes

    ~ 1 **cup dry lentils**

- The sausages from 3 above
- 1/2 **tsp basil**
- 1/2 **tsp marjoram**
- 1/2 **tsp sugar**
- 2 **bay leaves**
- 1/2 **tsp garlic salt**
- **salt** and **pepper** to taste

5. Bring to **BOIL,** then **SIMMER** 40 to 50 minutes until lentils are tender

ABOUT TOMATOES

Tomatoes came **to** Europe not **from** Europe. Many Europeans brought with them to America a suspicion that tomatoes were not edible and might even be poisonous. So the soups in this collection which have tomatoes in them cannot precisely be called soups that came from Bohemia. They are, however, soups that the Barron House fabricated using Bohemian cooking skills **and** an additional available ingredient that turned out to be both edible and useful.

The very positive reaction of the Barron House clientele to menu items which contained tomatoes encouraged The Barron House cooks to adapt, and to enlarge their repertoire. I do maintain that soups are an art form. I also encourage you to be inventive and artful.

John Bohumil

THE TOMATO SOUP

To this day, my sentimental favorite among tomato-type soups is one served often at the Barron House. Most of the Barron House soups were made from fresh ingredients. However, Campbell's original tomato soup was a staple on the House's pantry shelves. Try serving it. You may be surprised!

1. **HEAT** to boiling, then **SIMMER** for 5 minutes

    ~ 1 10 1/2 **oz can** of **Campbell's traditional Tomato Soup**

    (not low fat, not anything, but traditional!)

    ~ 1 1/2 **cans** of **whole milk**

2. **SERVE** in a bowl with

    ~ a 1/2 **TBSP** pat of **real butter** floated on top

I like the taste of butter floating on the milky tomato soup. Sometimes I drop a few oyster crackers split in half, into the butter waves as they float out from the butter pat. It is Bohemian-American heaven at the dining table! But, alas, it is an exception to my avowed promise of ingredients that are heart healthy!

FRESH TOMATO SOUP

When too many tomatoes ripened at once in the Barron House garden there was the choice of making tomato juice or tomato soup. The latter was a little easier and fit in well with the need for variety in soup courses. Frankly, this is a very easy and quick to make recipe for today's gardener. It also has the advantages of not being too tomato intensive and being very heart healthy.

1. **HEAT** to boiling and **SIMMER** for 15 minutes

    ~ 3 **cups** chopped **tomatoes** with skins

    ~ 3 **cups water**

    ~ 1/2 **cup** chopped **onion**

    ~ 1 **packet G. Wash Brown Broth**

    (or 2 beef flavored bouillon cubes)

    ~ 1 **packet G. Wash Golden Broth**

    (or 2 chicken flavored bouillon cubes)

    ~ 1/2 **cup** chopped **fresh parsley**

2. **LIQUEFY** in blender

3. **HEAT** again to boiling with

    ~ 2 **cups skim milk**

    ~ 1/2 **cup dry non-dairy cream**

John Bohumil

SUPERB TOMATO SOUP

Winters in Pennsylvania can be miserable. It was not unusual during the November to March period for the work crews that bedded down at the Barron House to spend the whole day outside in freezing rain or blowing snow. On days like that, the Barron House liked to serve this soup. It was put in the silver tureen and coddled on the hot bricks on a side table in the hotel dining room. The bricks were replaced every ten minutes to keep the soup as hot as possible. It was served in heavy mugs, which the waitresses kept filling during the meal until each diner said "Enough".

In an iron pot on your Vermont Casting wood stove, with winds howling outside and snow swirling down, this soup can be a perfect beginning for your dinner guests.

1. **Heat** to boiling

    ~ 2 10 1/2 **oz** undiluted cans of **Campbell's tomato soup**

    (or a similar brand)

    ~ 2 10 1/2 **oz** undiluted cans of **Campbell's Beef Consommé**

    ~ 1 **tsp sugar**

    ~ 1 **bay leaf**

    ~ 1/2 **tsp oregano**

The Barron House used Campbell's tomato soup and its own homemade dark brown beef broth. I don't know how they made the broth, but the use of Campbell's Consommé together with the other ingredients produces the taste of what they served. The version I'm including here was given to us by Pat Reynolds of Kensington, Maryland in the 1950's and we've enjoyed it ever since.

WINTER SQUASH SOUP

This soup was a big hit at the Barron House after Prohibition ended. The cooks liked it, too, because they could use whatever squash they had, and winter squash "keeps" for months!

1. **PEEL** and **SEED** 2 to 3 **pounds** of **winter squash** (half butternut and half acorn is a good combination, but others are fine)

2. **CUT** squash into 1/4 inch thick pieces and **FRY** on both sides in

    ~ 1/2 **olive oil** and

    ~ 1/2 **vegetable oil**

3. **IN ANOTHER PAN, FRY** in 2 **TBSP olive oil**

    ~ 2 **TBSP** chopped **onion**

    ~ 1 **tsp** chopped **garlic**

    ~ 1/4 **tsp thyme**

    ~ 1 **Bay leaf**

    ~ 1/2 **tsp paprika**

4. **ADD** 1/2 **cup dry white wine** to onion mix and **COOK** until liquid is reduced in half

5. **ADD** 16 **oz** diced or chopped **canned tomatoes** and **HEAT** to boiling

6. **CHOP** fried squash into small chunks and **ADD** to onion/wine/tomato mix

7. **ADD**

    ~ 8 **oz tomato sauce**

    ~ 1/4 **lb** grated **American** or **cheddar cheese**

    ~ 4 **cups G. Wash. Brown Broth** or 4 cups beef broth

- ~ 1 1/2 **cups water**
- ~ 1 **TBSP parsley**
- ~ 3/4 **tsp thyme**

8. **HEAT** until all cheese is melted

Sometimes the cooks also added one cup of cooked rice in step 7 for variety's sake. Feel free to do so.

THE GREAT DEPRESSION

The Great Depression, beginning in 1929 and extending to the beginning of World War II, impacted heavily on the Barron House.

During the early 1930's more men came to the back door of the Barron House looking for work or at least a bit of food than came through the front door as patrons. The "waste not want not" approach of the proprietor and his staff meant that the Barron House pinched and stretched so that no one ever left without food.

Sometimes there was work available. And local unemployed men would be hired for the day, their pay being breakfast and lunch and food for their whole family for supper. Sometimes the problem of transporting the food home (like soup, for instance) was a real challenge. But lard pails had lids and handles and the youngsters in the family would return them sparkling clean on their way to school the next day. Sauerkraut cans were big and good for food transport. Dixie cups helped. The Barron House in 1930 added a large outdoor swimming pool with a small restaurant that sold ice cream, hot dogs, burgers, candy, sodas, and Dixie cups were available from there.

Each day, it seemed, one or more men would come to the Barron House because food would always be provided.

Some would ask to sleep overnight in the Hotel's sheds. Others would share the town's jail to be out of the rain and cold.

For the proprietor, these circumstances seemed not unlike what Europe had been experiencing prior to his bringing his family to America. That experience meant that he and his family of cooks knew how to feed many out of little . . . and they did.

If you will look back at the soups in this volume you will see one way in which this was done, i.e. making soup count.

It was also during these years that Nat Warsaw, the entrepreneur, restarted the clothing factory down the street. He employed many of the townsfolk, mostly women. That was a blessing to many families. His factory was across the street from the Barron House's state-of-

John Bohumil

the-art swimming pool. The pool was unbelievable. Its bottom and walks were cement. Its filtering and chlorinating systems were so good the 35 yard by 75 yard swimming pool water would meet state drinking water standards <u>when</u> <u>full</u> <u>of</u> <u>swimmers</u>.

Nat Warsaw, who understood that many of his workers could not "waste" their money to pay the 15 cent swimming fee, arranged with the Barron House proprietor (by paying a flat summer fee) to get them "free" swimming any day the wanted.

It's true there were government programs designed to help people . . . but there were also helpers like Nat and the Barron House.

I've written this to precede the last batch of soup recipes. All of these which follow can be classified as Pennsylvania Dutch recipes. Each one, in its own way, illustrates how stomachs (especially of children) were kept from aching during difficult times.

BARLEY SOUP

Barley has always been a nutritious stomach filler. This recipe uses one group of vegetables and is very palatable. But in Depression times what was available was used.

The soup stock, then of course, was made from the proverbial soup bones.

1. **BOIL** 1/4 **cup** of **pearl barley** in 2 **cups** of **water** for 2 minutes

2. **COVER** tightly and let set for one hour

3. **MICROWAVE** until soft

    ~ 1/4 **cup** chopped **celery**

    ~ 1/4 **cup** chopped **carrots**

    ~ 1/4 **cup** chopped **onion**

    ~ 1/4 **cup** chopped **green or red pepper**

4. <u>After the hour,</u> **MIX** together

    ~ the barley and its water

    ~ the vegetables

    ~ 4 **cups** of **G. Wash. Brown Broth** or 4 cups beef bouillon

5. **SIMMER** 20 to 30 minutes

John Bohumil

CHIPPED BEEF SOUP

Sometimes something a little different can make the "same old thing" much more palatable. One of my close friends as an adult told me he hated turnips. He said that when he was a youngster (as I was) during the Depression his father could not get work or any income. But he was able to work for three months for a farmer who could only pay him in turnips and a few potatoes.

1. **FRY** in 3 **TBSP margarine** or **light butter** until soft

    ~ 3 **TBSP** chopped **onion**

    ~ 3 **TBSP** chopped **green pepper**

2. **ADD**

    ~ 2 **TBSP flour**

    ~ 2 **cups skim milk**

    ~ 1/4 **cup dry non-dairy creamer**

    ~ 1/2 **TBSP** chopped **parsley**

    ~ 1/4 **tsp paprika**

    ~ 2 **packets G. Wash. Golden Broth** or 2 chicken bouillon cubes

    ~ 2 **oz** of **chipped beef**, rinsed to remove salt, and torn into small shreds.

3. **BRING TO BOIL** and **SIMMER** for 5 minutes

Families learned to take the same ingredients they had to use over and over again and make them different by adding something unusual. This was that kind of recipe.

The Barron House Soups

PRETZEL SOUP

Think about a hungry youngster and about telling him he can eat a whole bunch of pretzels so long as he dunks them in milk. That might just take the "drab" out of his day.

1. **HEAT** to boiling a **cup** of **whole milk**, or skim for each serving

2. **ADD** 3/4 **TBSP** of **butter**, for each serving

3. **BREAK UP** thin salted **pretzels** into a bowl with the milk and butter

The Pennsylvania Dutch made and still make soft pretzels. Today these are available frozen. You lightly wet the top of the frozen pretzel, shake coarse salt on it and bake briefly (1 minute or so) in a microwave. The Pennsylvania Dutch used the soft. I like the hard thin ones.

John Bohumil

RIVEL SOUP

There has probably never been a Pennsylvania Dutch or Amish cook book printed without a Rivel soup recipe. Rivel soup really fills up the stomach.

1. **HEAT** 8 **cups** of **chicken** or **beef broth** to boiling (or use G. Wash. Golden Broth or Brown Broth)

2. **MIX**

   ~ 1 beaten **egg**

   ~ 1/2 **tsp salt**

   ~ 1 **cup flour**

3. Keep the broth boiling and rub the flour/egg mix through your hands into the broth trying to keep the forming lumps small

4. **ADD** 3/4 **cup** of **creamed corn** or mashed fresh corn cut off the cob

5. **SIMMER** for 10 minutes or so

6. For adults, **SEASON** with **pepper**

Most Rivel soup recipes have a higher proportion of flour to fewer cups of broth. I prefer the thinner version. You may not.

TOMATO MUSHROOM SOUP

This is another one of those easy to make, easily available ingredients soups.

But it has a dramatic finish.

1. **FRY** in 2 **TBSP** of **butter** or **margarine**

    ~ 2 **cups** of thinly sliced **mushrooms** (you may prefer chopped, after making it once)

2. **ADD**

    ~ 1 **cup tomato sauce** (canned)

    ~ 1 1/2 **cups skim mild** and 1/4 **cup dry non-dairy creamer**

3. **HEAT** to boiling in a pan twice the size of the liquid

4. **ADD** 1/2 **tsp baking soda**

5. **HEAT** again until soup foams up (a half minute or so)

6. **IT'S READY TO EAT** (notice the unusual texture of the soup)

John Bohumil

'WHITHER THE BARRON HOUSE

Time moves on. World War II took the Barron House workers (and many of its patrons) off to war or war-related jobs. The swimming pool had subsisted on customers driving to it in automobiles. Gas rationing put a stop to that, so the pool closed.

The Barron House did not go on to become a prosperous hotel chain. Like its swimming pool, it also closed.

And so the last recipe in this volume speaks of the good of the Barron House and of the good of the place where it existed. It is not a recipe brought from Bohemia, or anywhere in Europe o r Asia. It is one born in America, probably in New England and served regularly at the Barron House. It features a special food indigenous to America. And it is a recipe which is a traditional part of the annual expression of appreciation for what America has given to those who came to it from distant places.

I commend it to you and those you hold dear.

The Barron House Soups

THANKSGIVING CORN CHOWDER

1. **MICROWAVE** until crisp 4 slices of real smoked lean **bacon**

2. **COOK** until soft in 3 **TBSP vegetable oil**

    ~ 1 1/2 **cups** chopped **white onion**

3. **COMBINE AND COOK** until potatoes are fork tender

    ~ the bacon crumbled up

    ~ the soft onion

    ~ 3 **cups** peeled and diced raw **potatoes**

    ~ 8 **cups** of **water**

4. **HEAT** in a separate pan over medium heat until thickened and smooth

    ~ 3 **TBSP light butter**

    ~ 1/4 **cup flour**

    blended together before adding milk

    ~ 2 **cups skim milk**

    ~ 1/4 **cup dry non-dairy creamer**

5. **MIX** together, bring to a **BOIL**, and **SIMMER** 20 minutes

    ~ the bacon, potato, onion mix from 3 above

    ~ the white sauce from 4 above

    ~ 1 **ten oz package** of **frozen kernel corn**

    ~ 1 **ten or twelve oz can** of **creamed corn**

    ~ 2 **cups** of diced fully cooked lean **ham**

    ~ 1/2 **tsp black pepper**

    ~ 1/2 **tsp mace**

- ~ 1/2 **tsp paprika**
- ~ 1 **tsp thyme**
- ~ 2 crumbled **bay leaves**
- ~ 2 **tsp salt**

6. **ADD** to finished soup

- ~ 1 **cup** crushed **Carr's Water Crackers** soaked in 1 **cup skim milk**

7. Taste the finished soup. If it is too thick or too salty, add water. If not salty enough, add salt.

8. Serves 8 generously

A GENERAL NOSTALGIC POSTSCRIPT

At the Barron House the bacon used was always from a slab of farm meat cured with salt and real hickory smoke.

As a favor to yourself (if you are someone who eats and uses bacon) search around until you can find a meat market which can still provide you with such a real hickory smoked slab. Pick out the leanest slab they have and have them slice it (the whole thing!)

Then:

a. Make a flat 8" x 12" base of several sheets of aluminum foil

b. Put on it one single layer of bacon, the pieces not touching

c. Cover with a sheet of plastic wrap.

d. Put on another layer. Cover.

e. Repeat until the whole slab makes a nice pile of layers.

f. Put the pile in a 2 gallon baggie and the baggie into your freezer.

You will have a wonderful stock of bacon. Bacon freezes well and can go right into the microwave frozen.

ABOUT THE AUTHOR

The author was part of the family that carried on the Barron House Restaurant business. As a youngster and teenager in the 1920's, 30's and 40's he was "kitchen help" for meals and banquets. When the Barron House added a large outdoor state-of-the-art cement swimming pool he worked in the pool's short order restaurant.

After being drafted at the age of 18 in WWII he returned to Princeton University to finish his undergraduate years. During these years he earned tuition money by managing the Princeton University campus center short order restaurant.

After college he went on to other occupational fields in Federal and State Governments. He kept his interest in cooking, however, and long before retirement from his career work set out to reproduce dishes from old Barron House recipes.

This hobby became almost an obsession. His goal became to develop recipes which would recreate the taste and structure of the Barron House dishes but with ingredients that would meet today's health protecting standards.

This first volume contains soups which are heart friendly. These are soups which provide the taste of the 20's, 30's, and 40's Barron House menus but keep cholesterol and fat at a minimum.

Printed in the United States
26204LVS00003B/205-207